MANAGER
MANAGE THYSELF

Patrick Olliffe

authorHOUSE®

AuthorHouse™
1663 Liberty Drive
Bloomington, IN 47403
www.authorhouse.com
Phone: 833-262-8899

Published by AuthorHouse 08/10/2021

ISBN: 978-1-6655-3439-0 (sc)
ISBN: 978-1-6655-3447-5 (e)

Library of Congress Control Number: 2021916191

Print information available on the last page.

This book is printed on acid-free paper.

CONTENTS

ACKNOWLEDGMENTS

Gratitude makes sense of our past, brings peace for today, and creates a vision for tomorrow.
—Melody Beattie

I owe a debt of gratitude to the many people I have worked beside, for, and with over my career while I was struggling to learn the practice of management—people who have inspired, prodded, supported, and pushed me along my path to understanding the value of organizational capability.

A special thanks goes to my wife and best friend, Trish, for her unwavering faith in me and her willingness to read my many drafts, proof them, and suggest key changes.

To my children, Patrick and Keri, and their families, and to my granddaughter Ruby—I want to make you proud of me.

To my longtime running partner and confidant, John Palmiere, who over the thousands of miles we logged together always listened, asked tough questions, and rarely questioned my sanity.

To my family, who often questioned my sanity—and for good reason.

Gratitude is also stored in my heart for Sergeant Bryson, Tom Carleton, Ed White, my Fort Knox instructors, Pete Graziotto, Ray Barbarow, Craig Stephen, Dave Ferguson, Sue Hoehl, Linda Crawshaw, Angela Costa, Dr. Thomas Lundquist, Lou Romito, John Caverno, Father Conboy, Christopher Vaughan, Charlie Logue, Paul V. Logue, Beth Milwid PhD, Bob Davenport, Tomeeka West, Jim Shuster, Frank Jans, Ian Oliveros, Sandi Hornyak, Bob Howard, Leslie Nettleman,

Patrick Boyle, Don Fedor, Tim Metcalf, Garner Miller, JP McCormick, Bert Mooney, Ed Banos, and Christopher Shanley.

I know I have missed some people whose influence was significant and remains in my heart. For this, I apologize.

INTRODUCTION

Take pride in your work at all times. Remember, respect
for an umpire is created off the field as well as on.

                                            —Anonymous

This book is dedicated to all the men and women I have been privileged
to know and to work with and for over the years—the managers who
practiced their careers with an eye to creating organizational capability.

As I began to think about writing this book, one particular
experience came to mind that would set the tone for my writing.

It happened while I was conducting a management session in a
manufacturing facility outside Philadelphia several years ago. We were
in a makeshift training room just off the production floor. It was the
third shift, and nobody wanted to be there—but they had to be. Their
president had brought us in to help them achieve their company's cost-
savings goals. The atmosphere was a bit testy.

As I started to discuss management, one of the more senior and
skeptical participants stopped me and said, "I don't want to know what
others have said. I want to know what you say management is, and then
maybe I'll listen to you."

I thanked him for his willingness to say what was on his mind.
Then, after a moment, I said, "Management is a career you practice,
and your success is measured by the organizational capability you create
in your wake."

I paused to let it take hold before I repeated it. He half-smiled,
nodded, and agreed to listen and participate.

It was not a spur-of-the-moment definition. I had been developing it for some time. As a member of an international consulting firm (APC Skills) specializing in supporting the implementation of production systems, I had observed countless management behaviors and identified many tools managers used to get their work done. Some managers had become quite effective at inventing workarounds complemented by their unique management styles that seemed to fit their organizations at the time.

Over many projects, I got to know managers in banks, restaurants, warehouses, production facilities, and repair shops, to mention but a few. I found very few managers who actively managed their career—quantitatively or qualitatively. I also found many managers who wanted to know more about managing their careers, especially qualitatively.

They didn't necessarily want to become general managers. They did, however, want to contribute their talents to the sustainability of their organizations. Although that was seen as important to them, personally and professionally, it seemed too far away. They wanted something closer to home. They wanted to develop capability in their team, their shop, their department—their organization within their organization.

Now that's something they could get their arms around. That was something they could learn by doing. Most were experiential learners (more about that later).

My focus on organizational capability grew from these experiences. Organizational capability gives practicing managers a simple and effective way to do the following:

- grow employee engagement
- reduce waste and lost time
- instill pride in the work their employees do for their customers
- manage their career

When confronted with a possible solution or opportunity, simply asking *Will that grow organizational capability?* allows practicing managers to grow personally and professionally from wherever they are—to manage themselves so they can better manage others.

This book is designed to provoke thought and action—especially action. As you review, reflect, and reform your practice of management, you will do so with an understanding of your perspective, your opportunities, your available strategic responses, and your tactical plan.

Consider choosing a partner who also has an interest in career management—someone who wants to grow. Choose someone who can assist your development, not sabotage it. Choose someone who listens well, talks little, and who can, without judgment, summarize what you are saying and feed it forward for you. This is an important element in your management practice. Choose wisely.

Consider reading Marshall Goldsmith's book *What Got You Here Won't Get You There* for greater understanding of the concept of *feedforward*.

CHAPTER 1

Is It Management or Leadership?

⋙

What's in a name? That which we call a rose by any other name would smell as sweet.
—Shakespeare's *Romeo and Juliet*

The meaning of this Shakespeare quote for practicing managers today is that the importance of a thing is because of the way it is, not because of what it is called. By some accounts, the practice of modern management can be traced back to the sixteenth-century study of low-efficiency and failed enterprises conducted by the English statesman Sir Thomas More. Since that time, management has had many definitions and perspectives, including the following:

- the organization and coordination of the activities of a business in order to achieve defined objectives
- the directors and managers who have the power and responsibility to make decisions and oversee the enterprise
- the process of dealing with or controlling things and people
- getting what you want done through people

Semantics aside, management and leadership are both about influence. They may be similar, but they are not the same.

Leadership, as described by Paul Hersey and Ken Blanchard in their influential book *Management of Organizational Behavior*, can

1

be thought of as an attempt to influence the behavior of someone else for whatever reason, be it personal, professional, ideological, financial, technical, social, or political. Management, they went on to write, can be thought of as a special kind of leadership in which the accomplishment of organizational goals is paramount, none more important than organizational capability.

I believe much of the confusion over leadership versus management is rooted in our industrial past and the separation of labor and management. The cultural stigma of being the boss is now our twenty-first-century challenge. Some thought leaders have championed the notion that "everybody is a leader" and suggested that this would engage employees, reduce turnover, and create financial strength, organizational cohesion, technical excellence, customer furtherance, and growth.

How to get these initiatives from the treetops to the grass roots has been the challenge for practicing managers. The emphasis on leadership versus management has distracted us from searching for a solution to the operational, strategic and purposeful problems practicing managers are confronted with today.

In large organizations, in keeping with their purpose, the board of directors sets the strategies and defines the policies, which are then carried out by the chief executive officer and the management team to sustain the organization. In smaller organizations, the process is the same, but the senior management team—or in some cases the owner—clarifies the purpose of the organization, sets strategic goals, writes policy, ensures retention and engagement of employees, and delegates responsibilities as needed to sustain the organization. The process is the same, but strategies and tactics are adapted to fit the life cycle of the organization.

Depending on your position in your organization's complex work-processing system (employee, supervisor, foreman, manager, director, vice-president, or president/CEO), the nature of your work doesn't change, only your scope. Work is still an activity involving mental, physical, and emotional effort done for somebody else in order to achieve a purpose. Organizational work, by extension, can be thought of as the physical, mental, and emotional effort done collectively by the members of an organization to meet the needs and wants of their customers at a profit level sufficient to meet the organization's ongoing needs while gaining the trust of lenders who make funds available with the expectation that those funds will be repaid, including any interest or fees.

If we unpack that definition, we can see that work has four domains—technical, financial, social, and customer furtherance—and these should be included in everyone's expectations. The nature of work does not change based on the position one holds, only its scope. It requires a constellation of competencies supported by a culture of customer creation and furtherance.

The practice of management is both an art and a science aimed at growing organizational capability to ensure organizational sustainability while achieving career goals. If we want to know what management is, we have to start with its purpose. And its purpose must lie outside itself. It must, in fact, lie inside the business itself, since management is an organ of the business.

Businesses and their industries are dynamic. Businesses must be able to anticipate where new opportunity is to be created in the future and need everyone to participate as an expectation of the job. There is, therefore, only one valid definition of management purpose: to further organizational capability. Organizational capability is the foundation of the business, for it keeps the business in existence.

Organizational capability can be thought of as using the collective competencies of one's organization to gain an advantage over its competitors. It is everything your organization does collectively well that improves sustainability and distinguishes you in the marketplace. It is the result of the talent you hire, the abilities you train to, and the effective use of your people in developing technical excellence, ensuring financial strength, fostering social cohesion, and universalizing customer furtherance. It is what leads us to define *management* as a career we practice, the success of which is measured by the organizational capability we create.

CHAPTER 2

Your Organization's Current and Future Worth

⁘

This is what you do. You make a future for yourself out
of the raw material at hand.
                                        —Michael Cunningham

Many thought leaders, investors, and practicing managers have argued
that in order to calculate a company's current and future worth, the
most important factors to consider are the quality, experience, and
competency of its managers. I am one of those people.

In a letter to shareholders of Berkshire Hathaway, Warren Buffett
and Charles Munger said they were looking for "elephant-sized"
acquisitions using their historical criteria, which included the following:

- a solid management team
- attractive returns
- strong upside potential
- a reasonable purchase price

We have long believed and championed the belief that in order
to evaluate a company's current and future worth, one of the most
important factors is the competency of its managers—their collective
knowledge, skills, and attitudes—which creates organizational capability
within their organizations.

The Cambridge English Dictionary defines *worth* as having a particular value to someone. Value, therefore, by definition, is determined by the importance a "someone" (manager, investor, customer, academic, employee) places on an organization for a desired end. Examples include the following:

- Investors value return on capital and growth.
- Managers value purpose, vision, trust, courage, and capability.
- Customers value low prices, high-quality products, quick service, and good after-sales service.
- Employees value opportunity, fair pay, and reasonable treatment.
- Academics value integrity.

Worth, then, is a many-faceted metric, and an evaluation of an organization's current and future worth depends on one's perspective. In this book, the focus will be on management's perspective of worth that contributes to their organization now and in the future. These include the following:

- their purpose (customer furtherance)
- their conditions (process) and tools (systems, methods, procedures)
- their competencies (collective knowledge, skills, attitudes)
- their values (vision, trust, courage, capability)

It is your management team, both line and staff, acting together in a coordinated way to create capability that sustains your organization. Each specialty and function comes with its own views and its own biases. Organizational capability is the one thing that can unite these biases to create current and future worth.

Easier said than done! As Steve Maraboli, PhD, wrote, "Everything is easier said than done. Wanting something is easy. Saying something is easy. The challenge and the reward are in the doing." I believe, and many contemporary thought leaders agree, that process mapping is a reasonable starting point for doing. As one general manager in a manufacturing plant in Indiana told me years ago, "They put generals on horses for a reason: it gives them a broader view. My process is my modern-day horse. It gives me a broader view."

Process mapping is a reasonable starting point for doing. Organizations with a well-developed and well-maintained process map generally create and maintain organizational capability well into the future. Those organizations that do it best are consistently the most successful.

Below is a sample high-level process map to guide you in developing a capability map for your organization, within your organization. Once done, look for areas of disconnect and possible failures. Consider setting priorities and forming cross-functional or multidisciplinary teams to take action to resolve those possible disconnects.

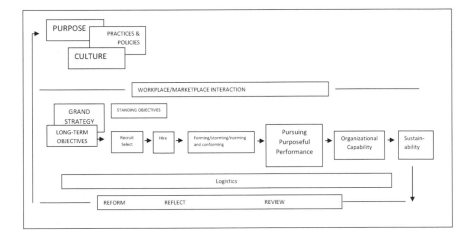

"Pursuing Purposeful Performance" is where it all comes together. It's where the action is and where your practice takes shape. It all starts upstream with the purpose of the organization. And as Peter Drucker wrote, its purpose must lie outside of the business itself. It must lie in society, since a business is an organ of society.

There is only one valid definition of business purpose: to create a customer. It is the customer who determines what a business is, for it is the customer—and the customer alone—who through a willingness to pay for goods or services converts economic resources into wealth and things into goods and services. The customer is the foundation of a business and keeps it in existence.

It is a vital system within your process, influenced by the upstream and downstream systems, methods, procedures, and metrics of your process. It can be thought of as a set of related subsystems that support your organizational capability process—simple, yet complex.

Oliver Wendell Holmes wrote, "I am not interested in simplicity on this side of complexity. I am only interested in simplicity on the other side of complexity." So should we be. Simplicity does not precede complexity. It follows it. Expect to be confused before you are informed. It takes trust and a commitment to your practice of management. In the words of Arthur Ashe, "Start where you are. Use what you have. Do what you can."

Start Where You Are

Start by identifying your workflow system. Determine where your work comes from (your supplier), what you do to it (add value), and where it goes when it leaves your shop (to your customer).

(IN)   (THROUGH)   (OUT)

Consider making your workflow system visible. Ask for other members' input. It's not truly valuable unless all stakeholders participate. It takes courage, perseverance, and curiosity. Consider your upstream influences, like how teams are formed before they perform; your strategic objectives; your market conditions; your purpose; and your culture.

Bruce Tuckman's model for team development can give you some insight into how a team forms, grows, affirms productive behaviors, faces up to challenges, tackles problems, finds solutions, plans work, and delivers results—in short, how teams pursue purposeful performance. Tuckman envisioned a forming, storming, norming, and performing model that has stood the test of time. I've added a fifth item, *conforming*, after seeing how many managers and teams assumed that setting norms was enough to ensure performance and paid little attention to whether team members truly conformed. Many managers and team members were unsure how to respond when norms were not being followed. Peer coaching was in its infancy, and many shied away from it because of its intrusive nature.

Use What You Have

No matter your position in the organization, you can create a process map for pursuing your team's purposeful work —the mental, physical, and emotional effort that contributes to your organization's purpose. Be prepared to change, to dispute outdated beliefs, and to face pushback. As Kurt Lewin theorized in his three-stage model of change known as *unfreezing*, *changing*, and *refreezing*, teams will need to let go of previous beliefs before they can change, and once changed, they will refreeze at a more sophisticated level—until the next challenge comes along.

Keeping your team members engaged, ready, and flexible while maintaining a high level of certainty can best be done by maintaining a focus on your immediate customer, the fourth domain of every organizational member's work. It has been said that systems support processes and processes support people. Mapping your work and applying key management values can make capability furtherance a daily occurrence.

As stated earlier, management values purpose, vision, courage, trust, and organizational capability to ensure sustainability. The following are some of the main elements of that philosophy:

- **Courage** in the face of risk is a choice managers make. As managers, we can choose to preserve the value we have already created, i.e. "move the organization along," or we can grow our team's capabilities even in the face of an uncertain marketplace.
- **Trust** in the expertise of your senior management team to create and communicate a clear, purposeful **vision** of the future. Trust in your employees' **willingness and ability** to support it. Trust in your competencies to develop the **capabilities** of your team.

- **Organizational capability** is the collective competency of your organization to gain an advantage over your competitors. It is everything your organization does collectively well that improves sustainability and distinguishes you in the marketplace. Capabilities are the result of the talent you hire, the abilities you train to, and the effective use of your people in customer furtherance, technical excellence, financial strength, and social cohesion.

Do What You Can

Your and your team's contribution to the organization's current and future worth is within your daily reach. By taking the above managerial steps, you can create a visual and realistic view of your organization's process that supports people and systems so you can reasonably contribute to your organization's current and future worth. *Start where you are. Use what you have. Do what you can.*

CHAPTER 3

Manager, Manage Thyself

Your time is limited, so don't waste it living someone else's life.

—Steve Jobs

His name was Michael Holland. He was somebody with presence, somebody you wanted to listen to. He was a big man who looked even bigger behind his desk—a desk that had a small bronze desk plate on it where most people had their nameplate.

His desk plate read, "Manager, Manage Thyself."

When asked about it (something you couldn't help but do if this was your first time in his office), he would finish the quote with, "so you can better manage others." He told me that when he ordered the desk plate, the company had a limit on the number of words he could put on it. Although initially disappointed, he grew to like the abbreviated version because it allowed him to finish it in person and add whatever story came to his mind at the time.

Michael left an indelible mark on me. Over the years, the most effective managers I have worked with and for all had a similar belief, but few expressed it as dramatically as Michael. That belief has been a staple of mine ever since I first encountered Michael, and I wanted to share it with you.

As practicing managers, we are sometimes so busy we forget this important belief—that is, until an event we attend reminds us. Think of a family reunion where good food and drink are plentiful and memories are repurposed to get a good laugh, usually at another family member's expense. Pictures are taken with promises to send them out to all in attendance. Eventually you get yours and start going through them. Who do you look at first? Be honest, now.

Sure, we tend to look at ourselves first. Then our eyes wander to others as we remember the important parts they have played in our lives. After a while, we are reminded of the value of family.

The same is true of management. When we attend a company retreat or offsite training event, there's usually a group photo taken to commemorate the event. I have several of them, and I'm sure you do too.

When you got your copy, or it was posted in the company newsletter, you went through a similar process of looking at yourself, then others, remembering their importance or challenges in your career, before settling on organizational purpose and the importance of organizational capability.

As you entered the world of work, most likely you did so from a technical/functional perspective, but as you progressed through your career, you made a decision to pursue a career in management. Your perspective changed from what MIT's Edgar Schein calls your technical/functional anchor to your management anchor. You may have gone from, or aspire to go from, a supervisor/foreman to a middle manager, or perhaps to a senior management position. Often, our work life becomes separated from our home and family life as we wait for the weekend to reset ourselves.

It doesn't have to be that way. In later chapters, I'll show you how, as you manage your career and earnestly listen to the encouragement, "Manager, manage thyself." To paraphrase Matthew McConaughey's Oscar acceptance speech in 2014, there are three things we need *every day* as a manager:

- something to look up to
- something to look forward to
- someone to chase

The *something to look up to* would be organizational capability. It is the art of the long view. The *something to look forward to* would be purposeful work—work that contributes to organizational capability and your professional sustainability anchored in what I call *work-centric*. By many accounts, looking forward to even the smallest things can make your day more enjoyable, improve your outlook, and lower your stress, which means better health for you as a practicing manager. What could be healthier than seeking reasonable anticipation of organizational and professional objectives, of learning from work, of living a purposeful life?

The *someone to chase* would be you in seven years—your predictive self. Predicting is stating something before its expected future date. Creating your predictive self can be best done by answering the following questions:

- What will your predictive self look like in seven years?

_____

_____

_____

_____

_____

_____

_____

_____

_____

- What would achieving this goal mean to you?

_____

_____

_____

_____

_____

_____

_____

_____

_____

_____

- What evidence will you have when you achieve this goal? What will you see, hear, and feel?

_____

_____

_____

_____

_____

_____

_____

_____

_____

- Where and with whom do you want to accomplish this goal?

_____

_____

_____

_____

_____

_____

_____

_____

_____

- What actions are you willing to take to achieve this goal?

_____

_____

_____

_____

_____

_____

_____

_____

_____

_____

- When you achieve this goal, what will be the impact on the other aspects of your life?

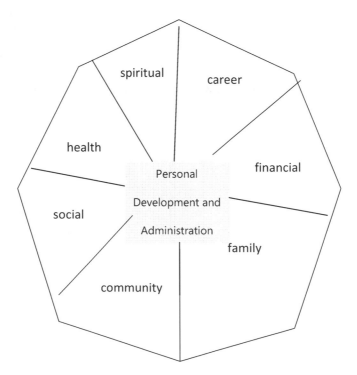

_____

_____

_____

_____

_____

_____

_____

_____

_____

_____

_____

_____

_____

_____

- Thinking back, what roadblocks got in the way of your goals?

_____

_____

_____

_____

_____

_____

_____

_____

- You already have great skills, tools, and resources. Which ones will help you achieve your predictive self?

_____

_____

_____

_____

_____
_____
_____
_____
_____
_____

- What other resources do you need to accomplish this goal?

_____
_____
_____
_____
_____
_____
_____
_____
_____
_____

- What action steps will you take to acquire these resources?

_____
_____
_____
_____
_____
_____
_____
_____
_____
_____

This is a good time to touch on time management in your practice of management. Time management is about achieving organizational goals by influencing yourself and others regarding the importance of doing one activity versus another. It's about going beyond *schedules* to build *relationships*; beyond *efficiency to* emphasize *effectiveness*; and beyond *control* to create *influence*

As Robert Collier, in his book *The Secret of the Ages,* wrote, "You may have anything you want in life provided that you:

- creatively decide what you want
- want it badly enough
- confidently expect to attain it
- continually decide to attain it
- are willing to pay the price of its attainment."

Or as Michael Holland advised so many years ago: "Manager, manage thyself so you can better manage others."

CHAPTER 4

Creating an Organizational Reputation

❦

You can't buy a reputation, you must earn it.
—Harvey Mackay, businessman, author, and
syndicated columnist

Earning a good management reputation requires consistency of effort and action. To repeat: Earning a good management reputation (*the general belief other people have of you as a manager*) requires consistency of effort (*the vigorous and determined attempt to understand management*) and action (*the practice of management to achieve an aim*).

So it begs the question: what is your aim? Maybe it's one of the following:

- to be efficient
- to keep a schedule
- to utilize your resources fully
- to be productive
- to comply with systems, methods, and procedures and ensure others do as well
- to learn and be popular
- to pursue your career
- to share responsibility

- to pursue purposeful performance
- to develop organizational capability for your organization within your organization

Your aim depends on many factors, including your earliest observations of managers, your technical/functional interests and talents, and whatever stage you find yourself at in your practice of management.

Are you in your initial management position, reestablishing yourself as a manager in a new organization, seeking to gain an organizational reputation, looking for a degree of job security, learning advanced skills, adjusting to changing conditions, finding new ways to contribute, or seeking to leave a legacy for younger managers? An observable growth pattern with inflection points, as we see it, would look like this:

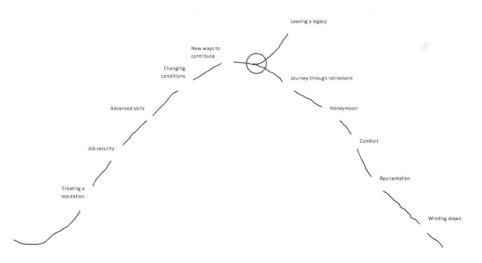

An inflection point (that point on a curve where a change in direction occurs) can happen at any career stage, none more significant than at the "new ways to contribute" stage, but we will explore that more deeply in a later chapter. No matter the stage, we are always learning. And for adults, arguably the most natural and powerful form of learning is through experience—what educational professionals call *experiential learning.*

John Kolb, one of the leaders in experiential learning, has described it as a system of practice, reflection, understanding, and repetition.

Adapting Kolb's model to the practice of management would give us a system like this:

But, as we have seen earlier, management systems don't live in a vacuum. They live in a process inductively designed to grow organizational capability that ensures sustainability for their organization.

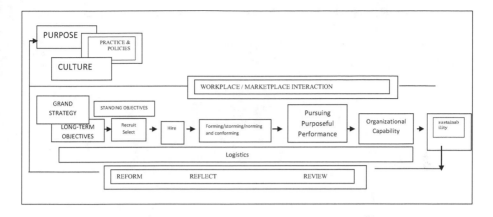

Pursuing (the effort to secure or attain) purposeful performance is at the heart of the practice of management. It is influenced by upstream forces, as displayed above, and creates downstream impact on organizational capability and sustainability. Said another way, purpose initiates process, systems support processes, and processes support people.

Although we manage locally, we need to think organizationally to create a good reputation. "We need to think about big things, while doing small things, so all the small things go in the right direction," as Alvin Toffler wrote. As a manager, the scope of your work gives you a broader view of your organization than that of your direct reports and can help you guide them to perform better.

Your metrics of performance are the starting point for your pursuit of performance and your *review, reflect, and reform* system and subsystems. That leads us to ask, "What is your *pursuit of performance* system—that group of interconnected and interactive parts that performs an important task as a component of a larger process?" Perhaps an example of a more representative and detailed system would help. Let's take a 35,000-foot view of your performance system.

PURSUIT OF PURPOSEFUL PERFORMANCE

PERFORMANCE
- purpose
- culture
- operations
- esxpectations
- problem-solving approach

REFORM
- make changes
- unfreeze, change, refreeze
- organizational capability
- organizational integration

REVIEW
- risks
- results
- problems

REFLECT
- investigate
- determine complexity
- deliberate

The three critical subsystems and their competencies are as follows:
- Operations
  - Know your operational subsystem.
  - Make it visual.
  - Discuss it.
- Setting reasonable expectations
  - Link expectations to organizational strategies.
  - Understand the nature of your work.
  - See your team members as individual contributors, not fungible resources.
  - Treat your people as the professionals they are.
- Problem-solving approach

o   Apply intuitive and systematic approaches appropriately.
o   Define the problem.
o   Set problem ownership.
o   Move from problem to objective.
o   Set contextual responses.

Your Operational Subsystem and Competencies

Your operational subsystem identifies where your work comes from, what you do to it to add value, where it goes when it leaves your area, and the probable competencies at each step.

IN	THROUGH	OUT
(Where it comes from)	(How you add value to it)	(Who gets it—internal/ external customer)

The Relevant Competencies for Each Step

IN	THROUGH	OUT
Assess	Further customer view	Quality product
Evaluate	Save resources	Well-served customer
Welcome	Reduce stress	Customer as ambassador
Classify	Know subsystems	Reliable service
Identify	Find economic opportunities	Organizational capability
Empathize	Evaluate in-process adjustments	Evaluate purposeful performance

Your *Reasonable Expectations* Subsystem and Competencies

Setting reasonable performance expectations for your team members is about stating how good or bad their behavior is supposed to be in a system of alignment, determination, and communications. Align your team's work with your organization's purpose and strategic objectives; determine how important each individual's contribution is and how important each team member is; and finally, communicate your expectations so your team knows what you expect and why.

Performance expectations are influenced by the marketplace, your industry, your organization, your customers, your employees, and the work itself. Activity involves the mental, physical, and emotional effort done for somebody to achieve a purpose. Unpacking that definition reveals work's four domains—technical, financial, social, and customer—and the basis for your expectations. Expectations can be thought of as the behaviors you expect to occur while your individual contributors work individually and collectively to accomplish their goals.

Most, if not all, organizations have some form of expectations for their members—line, staff, union, management, or professionals—that generally include the following no matter how they frame and present them:

- dependability
  - capable of being trusted; to think, learn, and participate in the work of the organization; to be available
- productivity
  - yielding results, benefits, economic opportunities, customer furtherance, or profits
- safety
  - occupational
    - avoiding biological, chemical, physical hazards, and practicing ergonomics
  - psychosocial
    - avoiding sexual harassment, victimization, and workplace violence
- maturity
  - being responsible for your actions; being sensitive and considerate toward others; and having the ability to change and adapt to changing circumstances

To be effective at setting reasonable expectations, now and into your future as a practicing manager, we suggest you start where you are. Take a look at the stated performance standards in your organization. Review them for omissions. Do they speak to the technical, financial, social, and customer domains of work? If not, do you see it as a problem or an opportunity?

John Adams, our country's second president, wrote: "Every problem is an opportunity in disguise." It takes an effective system and well-developed competencies to see beyond the disguise; to identify the problem accurately; and to set objectives for your organization within your organization.

Problem-Solving Subsystem and Competencies

"Problems, problems, problems! Doesn't anybody have any solutions?" was the lament of the frustrated senior director of logistics when I talked with him about his department. When I asked him what that meant, his answer was telling: "It seems I fix a problem, but it never stays fixed for very long."

He prided himself as a man of action but sensed something was not working. He wanted some suggestions for fixing things in a way that actually stuck. It would be challenging to get him to see that he would need to apply different approaches to different types of problems. His favorite *act—sense—respond* approach was not working for him or his team. It seemed to work only for the most chaotic situations, which, he admitted, were rare.

As practicing managers building our management reputation, we can learn much from that senior director's lament. First, we can learn that not all problems we encounter put the same pressure on us to perform. Second, it would be useful to have a framework to help us make sense of the different types of problems we encounter, depending on how predictable or unpredictable they are.

In the early 2000s, I began reading about such a system developed by IBM's David Snowden in the late 1990s. I never saw it as a guarantee of success but rather a guide for avoiding an overreliance on my intuitive style, which worked sometimes but not all the time. I believe it can help any practicing manager intent on building a good reputation now and into the future.

Snowden and his team titled it the Cynefin model. *Cynefin* is a Welsh word meaning a sense of place, a context. This framework, applied to organizational capability, sorts the issues facing managers into five contexts defined by the nature of the relationship between cause and effect. Four of these—*simple, complicated, complex,* and *chaotic*—require managers to observe situations and to act in contextually appropriate ways. The fifth—*disorder*—applies when it is unclear which of the other four contexts is predominant and gathers more information to identify it.

Using the Cynefin framework can help managers determine which context they are in so that they can not only make better decisions but also avoid the problems that arise when their preferred problem-solving style causes them to make mistakes.

Simple Context: The Domain of Best Practice

Simple contexts are characterized by stability and clear cause-and-effect relationships. Properly assessed, simple contexts require straightforward management and monitoring. Here, leaders *sense—categorize—respond.*

Using established practices is common, and often appropriate, in simple contexts. Difficulties arise, however, if employees are discouraged from questioning the process even when it's not working anymore.

Complicated Context: The Domain of Managing Experts

Complicated contexts, unlike simple ones, may contain multiple right answers, and though there is a clear relationship between cause and effect, not everyone can see it. While leaders in a simple context must *sense—categorize—respond* to a situation, those in a complicated context must *sense—analyze—respond*.

This context often requires outside expertise before managers can make a decision challenging them to manage the experts. Expect pushback. Experts have, after all, invested much in building their knowledge, and they are unlikely to be open to challenging ideas. To get around this issue, the practicing manager will need to listen to the experts while simultaneously welcoming fresh thoughts and solutions from other stakeholders. Reaching decisions in the complicated domain can take time, and there is always a trade-off between finding the best answer and simply making a decision.

Setting an objective up front, with an expected completion date, and confirming how a decision will be made is an effective way to deal with this common issue. We'll talk more about in a later chapter. When the best answer seems to be elusive, however, and you must base your decision on incomplete data, your situation is probably *complex* rather than *complicated*.

Complex Contexts: The Domain of Emergence

In a complicated context, at least one right answer exists. In a complex context, however, right answers can't be ferreted out using simple or complicated approaches.

To paraphrase what I recently read about this context, it's like the difference between a static machine and the marketplace. Ferraris are complicated machines, but a team of expert mechanics can take one apart and reassemble it without changing a thing. The car is static, and the whole is the sum of its parts. The marketplace, on the other hand, is in constant flux. A product or service becomes extinct, buying patterns change, an invention reroutes an industry, and the whole is far more than the sum of its parts.

This is the domain to which much of contemporary business has shifted and is challenging your reputation. Situations in organizations become complex because some major change or pending change introduces unpredictability and flux. In this domain, managers can almost always understand why things happen in retrospect. But as observers, practicing managers can prospectively begin to see patterns emerging.

That is why, instead of attempting to impose a course of action, managers must patiently allow the path forward to reveal itself. They need to probe first, then sense, and then respond. Understanding what a problem is can be an important part of being a practicing manager as you work to develop a good reputation.

Let me share a problem definition with you that can change the trajectory of your reputation for years to come. Credit goes to Dorothy Craig and her *Hip Pocket Guide to Planning and Evaluation.* Dorothy wrote, "A problem is a situation or condition of people or the organization that will exist in the future and is considered undesirable by the members of the organization."

Let me repeat that: "A problem is a situation or condition of people or the organization that will exist in the future and is considered undesirable by the members of the organization." The most important part of this definition is to think of the problem as something that will happen in the future if nothing is done. It is not a simple context nor a complicated context, but rather a complex one.

As in the other contexts, practicing managers face several challenges in the complex domain. Of primary concern is the temptation to fall back into using your favorite style and to demand failsafe business plans with defined outcomes. Practicing managers who don't recognize that a complex domain requires a more observational mode of management may become impatient when they don't seem to be achieving the results they were aiming for quickly enough. If they try to over-control their organization from within their organization, they will preempt the opportunity for informative patterns to emerge.

Leaders who try to impose order in a complex context will fail. Those who set the stage, step back a bit, allow patterns to emerge, and determine which ones are desirable will succeed. They may recognize many opportunities for innovation.

Chaotic Context: The Domain of Rapid Response

In a chaotic or crisis context, searching for right answers would be pointless. The relationships between cause and effect are impossible to determine because they shift constantly and no manageable patterns exist—only turbulence. The events of September 11, 2001, fall into this category.

In the chaotic domain, a practicing manager's immediate job is to stop the bleeding, not to discover emerging patterns. A practicing manager must first act to establish order, then sense where stability is present and from where it is absent, then respond by working to transform the situation from chaos to complexity, where the identification of emerging patterns can both help prevent future crises and recognize new opportunities. Communication of the most direct top-down kind is imperative; there's simply no time to ask for input.

Much has been written about the events of September 11. They were not immediately comprehensible, but the crisis demanded decisive action. Many reported that New York's mayor at the time, Rudy Giuliani, demonstrated exceptional effectiveness under chaotic conditions by issuing directives and taking action to reestablish order. However, in his post-crisis role as mayor, he was widely criticized by these same people for maintaining that same top-down leadership style that proved so effective during the emergency.

A specific danger for practicing managers following a crisis is that some of them become less successful when the context shifts because they are not able to switch styles to match it.

Practicing Management Across Contexts

Effective management requires openness to change on an organizational and an individual level. Truly practiced managers will know not only how to identify the context they're working in at any given time but also how to change their behavior and their decisions to match that context while preparing their organization, from within their organization, to understand the different contexts and the conditions for transition between them.

In the complex environment of the current business world, an understanding of context, the ability to practice management across contexts, and a willingness to change management style will be required for managers who want to build organizational capability within their organization.

CHAPTER 5

Acquiring Advanced Competencies

Strategy without tactics is the slowest route to victory. Tactics without strategy is the noise before defeat.

—Sun Tzu

To the wise words above from the ancient Chinese general and influential military strategist, we would humbly add that either, without a meaningful purpose, is a waste of talent. It's the *why* we do that comes before the *what* we do and *how* we do it.

Several years ago, I was walking around the shop floor of a large repair facility with the recently promoted director when he suddenly stopped, turned to me, and proudly stated, "I am the best blankety-blank foreman this company ever had."

I'll admit I was taken by surprise. What I wasn't surprised by was that in less than a year, he was gone. Unfortunately, he had remained a foreman while acting in the capacity of a director. He was enhancing what was, not advancing toward what could be. He lacked an awareness of his organization's meaningful purpose and his contribution to it, and a strategy for acquiring advanced competencies (the knowledge, skills, and attitude) of a director.

His was not the only talent I saw go wasted over the years. There were many examples. The industry, the section of the country, the age, the gender of the incumbent, or the life cycle of the organization did not seem to matter. Talent waste took many forms—from quiet compliance,

31

to retirements in place with a "you can't fight city hall" attitude, to premature resignations, and unfortunately to some needless discharges.

It became apparent to me as I crisscrossed the country in the go-go stage of my career as a member of an international consulting firm that too many managers reached a point in their careers of satisfaction or acquiescence and stopped being curious, stopped learning, stopped acquiring more advanced management competencies, and started supporting the status quo. As the late futurist Alvin Toffler wrote, "The illiterate of the 21st century will not be those who cannot read and write, but those who cannot learn, unlearn, and relearn."

Unlearning—or unfreezing, as Kurt Lewin referred to it in his three-step change model (unfreeze, change, refreeze)—can feel unsettling and is often avoided or quietly resisted. Unlearning, change, and relearning need a focus, something that inspires managers to manage in the short term while thinking about the long term so all the short-term activities go in the right direction.

Perhaps you have heard of the inspirational story of the three bricklayers. As the story goes, a man was walking down the street when he saw three bricklayers at work. Curious, he asked the first one, "What are you doing?"

"I'm laying bricks," the first bricklayer said gruffly.

Coming upon the second, the man asked the same question.

"I am building a wall," this bricklayer responded.

Impressed, the man asked the third bricklayer the same question.

The third man said, with enthusiasm and pride, "I'm building a cathedral."

It has been suggested that we can learn much from this short and simple story of the three bricklayers. We can learn about one of the core secrets of success: motivation. We hear a lot about the third bricklayer. Many tout the importance of that bricklayer's attitude and his ability to conceive a larger purpose. What we often don't hear about is the fourth bricklayer—the forgotten bricklayer.

When asked what he was doing, the fourth bricklayer, we'll call him John, replied, "I am building a cathedral where the community can come together and worship."

John knew who his customers were and how what he did would benefit them. He understood his work in all its domains: technical, financial, social, and customer. John went on to become the foreman of that team of bricklayers. He would often ask his team, "What do you think the community will see in our cathedral? Who are the people who will come? What do they think, feel, do, or say? How much better do you think their community will be because of what we are doing today?"

After becoming foreman and building a successful team, our now not-so-forgotten fourth bricklayer experienced an inflection point and decided he could make a greater contribution to his organization and grow his career by seeking to become a manager, to build on the reputation he had developed for customer furtherance and organizational capability by working with other managers. He realized he would need to acquire advanced skills. He would need to change.

In the previous chapter, we stressed the importance of unfreezing our attitude about work, especially "the somebody" our team does it for. *Hint, hint.* It is the customers, the customers, always the customers, whatever you happen to call them—patients, clients, internal or external customers, consumers, parishioners, or constituents. Customer identification and furtherance becomes more complex the broader one's view becomes, from frontline manager to middle manager to senior management. The problems of customer identification need advanced competency beyond categorizing and analysis.

Sure, maybe John's well-developed original approach of *sense— categorize—respond* worked for his team's simple and obvious issues. Maybe his analytical approach of *sense—analyze—respond* worked for his team's complicated issues. But as his view of the organization broadened and he interacted with people outside his functional area of responsibility on a more regular basis, his issues would become more complex. He would be challenged to develop a more complex way of resolving them.

John needed to master a complex approach of *probe—sense—respond* to complement his existing approaches. David Snowden's Cynefin framework, which we spoke about earlier, would be helpful. To probe is to ponder and to unfreeze our familiar and habitual thinking. We need to develop an advanced competency, a discriminating competency. We need to differentiate between the obvious, the complicated, and the complex to avoid the organization within our organization lapsing into ineffectiveness.

You've developed some core competencies while building your reputation. Build on them. To continue to build on that reputation, you'll need to acquire some advanced, contextual competencies to work with other functional experts in a cross-functional way. Most likely, your experience in cross-functional teams will begin as a participant. The team leader will form the team and explain its purpose, timeframes, and ground rules, and answer any questions that may be on the minds of participants in an initial meeting.

Depending on the sophistication of the team, you may be asked to be a note-taker or timekeeper. Additionally, your team leader may have engaged a facilitator who will act as the moderator to ensure every voice is heard and the process is followed. As mentioned in an earlier chapter, teams go through a maturing process from forming to storming, norming, and conforming before performing. Expect the same for your team. Observe, participate, and learn. The cross-functional experience can be an important inflection point in acquiring advanced skills.

A review of the cross-functional writings of management thought leaders, contemporary and historical, can feel overwhelming. There is so much to learn. I found the writings of Robert Katz to be helpful and insightful. He wrote that there are three core skills of management: conceptual, human, and technical. The extent of their application may vary by one's level of responsibility, but they are present at all levels. Here is a quick review of Katz's work. It reinforces the *why, what, and how* approach that is critical for developing advanced skills aimed at organizational capability and career management in the following ways:

- **Conceptual Skills: Why We Do It**
  These skills involve the ability, the knowledge, and the attitude for managers to use abstract thinking and formulate ideas. The manager is able to see an entire concept, analyze and diagnose

a problem, and find creative solutions. This competency helps managers to effectively predict hurdles their department or the business as a whole may face; to take in the big picture of the entire organization; and to use abstract ideas to set strategic initiatives.

- **Technical Skills: What We Do**
  Technical skills involve the ability, the knowledge, and the attitude needed for managers to use a variety of techniques to achieve their objectives. These competences not only involve operating machines and software, production tools, and pieces of equipment but also the skills needed to boost sales, design different types of products and services, and market the services and products; and also to accomplish tasks for those working on the front lines, their techniques, practices, tools, and processes.

- **Human Skills: How We Do It with Others**
  These skills involve the ability, the knowledge, and the attitude for managers to interact, work with, or relate effectively with people. These skills enable managers to make use of people's potential and motivate employees for better results. These skills involve communication and attention to relationships with others.

Managerial Skills According to Robert Katz

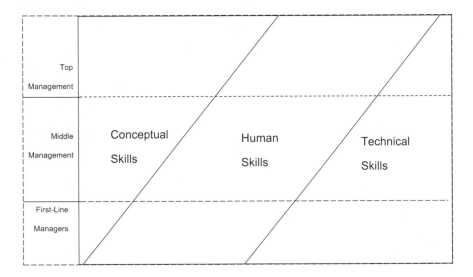

In a cross-functional team setting, practicing managers experience advanced skill development in dealing with complex priorities and competing ideas. Participants are challenged to express their organizational views with other practicing functional managers. Their technical and human skills will be tested. This is where the value of a facilitator can be seen. A facilitator ensures all voices will be heard, not just those with the greatest knowledge, highest position, or loudest volume.

An advanced technical support method I observed while at Allegheny General Hospital, designed to ensure that every member's voice was heard, was MERIDIA's electronic voting technology. I was introduced to it at as a member of the management council of a large teaching hospital where it was demonstrated. Although the hospital decided not to invest in the technology at the time, its value was immediately evident to me. If used purposefully, it can lessen tension, enhance decision-making, and increase engagement. Organizational capability can be continuously developed when conceptual skills are valued, facilitated, and supported by technical advancements.

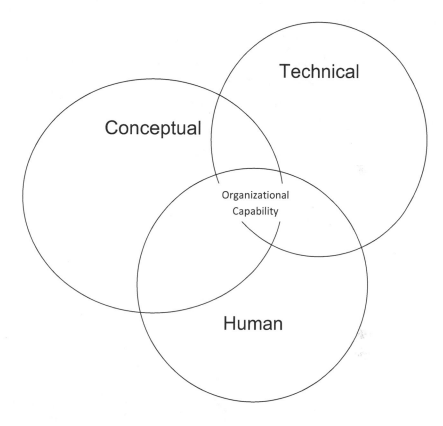

With so many advantages why do so many cross-functional teams fail? They fail, at a minimum, because of the following:

- an incomplete process
- poor facilitation—the ranking manager attempts to act as the facilitator and contributor
- used as brainstorming activity, not a problem-solving activity
- no timekeeping role assigned
- no note-taking role assigned
- failure to properly sunset the team—no after-team review, reflection, or reform, to mention but a few.

Let's end this chapter where we began, remembering that "Strategy without tactics is the slowest route to victory. Tactics without strategy is the noise before defeat." To these wise words from that ancient Chinese general and influential military strategist, we would humbly add that either, without a meaningful purpose, is a waste of talent.

Invest your talents in your management career. It is a noble endeavor—something you practice, where success is measured by the organizational capability you create in your wake.

CHAPTER 6

Being Prepared for Changing Conditions

Just when I think I have learned the way to live, life changes.

—Hugh Prather, PhD

Markets change, customers want and need change, employees change, management responds, organizations take action, individual contributors react, and career adjustments are often necessary. We can think of our career as a figurative journey through learning, work, and other aspects of life. The word *career* comes from the Latin word *carrus*, referring to a chariot, a vehicle, a way to travel a course to one's destination. Over time, it came to mean the course of one's public or professional life.

The word is used in a variety of ways—both as a noun and a verb. As a noun, it often refers to an occupation undertaken for a significant period of a person's life and with opportunities for progress, such as a profession, an occupation, a vocation, an anchor, or a position. As a verb, it means to move swiftly and in an uncontrolled way in a specified direction; for example, "Her career careered when she was downsized."

Good careers don't just happen. Like most important things, they have to be managed. Think about when you have friends over for dinner: to make a good meal, you must plan what you're going to have, get the food, cook it, adjust to changing conditions, enjoy the process, serve to family and friends, and take pride in the reputation you are building as a good host or hostess. To have a good career, you must also plan, make good choices, adjust when necessary, work conscientiously, get in step with the process, and take pride in the reputation you are building as a practicing manager.

A good career takes longer to plan than a good social gathering around a meal. In-process adjustments are sometimes painful. Hard work and adjustments may not be fun, but they can lead to good things.

Here I want to talk about being prepared to make adjustments for predictable career transitions—internally or externally motivated—as we respond to life's changes. In short, it's a process of capturing your perspective, position, and performance.

It begins with your *perspective*, your individual point of view, your management career anchor. This includes recognition of your current *position*, the clarity of your current place and the systems and competencies you use to keep you focused, and your *performance* aimed toward your future objectives. You'll need a *strategy* to guide your progress and *tactics* to direct your career with its predictable transitions as you integrate it into your daily life.

At 35,000 feet, it would look like this.

GETTING IN STEP WITH CHANGING CONDITIONS

A COMPLEX VENTURE

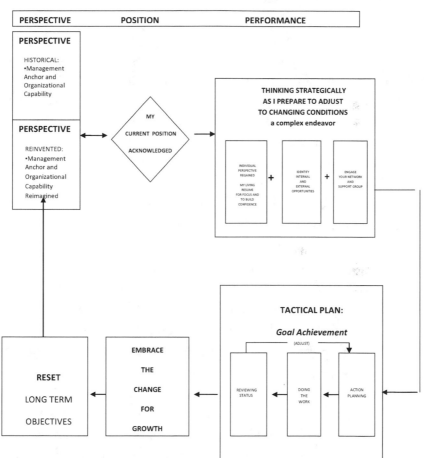

Take a moment and think back to when you first entered management:

- What did you see in the opportunity?
- Did you develop a résumé that distinguished you from your competition? Was it something you grabbed off the internet, or did you put some work into it to present yourself clearly in print?
- Were you able to actively participate in the interview?

- And, most importantly, after you got that position, did you put your résumé away for some future time when a new management opportunity presented itself?

If you answered *yes* to that last question, I have to ask, why? Your résumé, like strategic planning, is both a process and a product. It is a diary of your successes, your disappointments, what you learned from them, and how you grew as a manager—keeping you in the chase, engaging your personal support team, and creating convergence, not bifurcation, of your work life and your personal life.

Sound impossible or at least improbable? I thought so too for the longest time. Then a routine encounter with a senior manager changed all that. Let me tell you the story that influenced my thinking as I was asking myself the same question—an analysis interview that changed my attitude and my approach and has guided my career ever since.

In early 1977, while a member of an international consulting firm, I interviewed the president of a large transportation company in Chicago to determine if we could save his organization some money by minimizing the lost time he was experiencing in his organization. I assured him our approach would engage his managers to participate in developing their site-specific system, take responsibility for implementing it, and keep improving it over time.

During our conversation, he offered some insight into how he manages his career. It was a remarkably simple and familiar approach of bringing together the professional and personal aspects of his life—of managing himself so he could better manage his career. He opened the right-hand drawer of his desk and pulled out his résumé. It was not a pristine document ready to be sent out but rather a foundational document with handwritten notes on it and dates of occurrences written in the margins.

"This is my diary of successes and disappointments," he said, "my living résumé. It keeps me focused. I keep it alive so I will be prepared when the next challenge comes along. I share it with my family and significant support group so they remain a part of it."

In his own way, he was reinforcing what I had been earlier advised to do: "Manager, manage thyself so you can better manage others." In his own practical way, he found something to look up to, something to look forward to, and someone to chase. But this story will be as lasting as a Sunday sermon unless we have a way to practice it—a process of career management for practicing managers.

So here is the how-to part of practicing your management career, where success is measured by the organizational capability you create in your wake with the cycle of career development running in the background. The cycle begins with a review of your career capabilities to set an attitude of "Yes I can, because I've earned the right." With that attitude, we constantly seek to understand management, from its legacy to its current state.

This is what leads us to say that management is a career we practice whose success is measured by the capability we create in our wake. We practice while learning to get better. Skills and competencies are expanded through a process of review, reflection, and reform as we develop career capabilities.

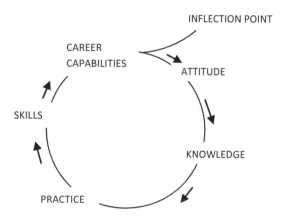

There are two macro ways to get your living résumé going if you don't have an up-to-date one: a tactical approach and a strategic approach. They both offer an extrospection and an introspection method, with costs and benefits for each. You can choose the one that works best for you.

The Tactical Way

- The *extrospection method* suggests you go online and use one of the many templates available, or go to your nearest bookstore and get the latest book on résumés.
- The *introspection method* suggests an analytical approach based on a review of your work history.

The Strategic Way

- The *extrospection method* suggests you engage a professional résumé-writing service. These generally begin with an initial information-gathering session that can take an hour or more depending on the extent of your background. This is followed by a week or so where they pull your information together into a professionally written résumé and invite you back for review and tentative approval. When this draft is updated and approved, they print as many copies and matching envelopes as you need.
- The *introspection method* suggests you use your analytical, synthesizing, and organizing skills to review your accomplishments and pull your skills from them. Once these are identified, prioritized, and written using action words, you can format your résumé from your reservoir of skills. This can take time and work, but the rewards are worth it.

TACTICAL		STRATEGIC	
EXTROSPECTIVE	**INTROSPECTIVE**	**EXTROSPECTIVE**	**INTROSPECTIVE**
Online templates as well as	Self-analytical approach	Résumé-writing services	Self-analytical approach
templates found in résumé	based on one's work	and career service	based on one's
books and workbooks	history	organizations	accomplishments and
			deduced skills

Whichever method you choose, your goal is to begin your living résumé as a reasonable way forward to "managing thyself." Because the strategic introspective approach is the most valuable for practicing managers, we will explain it here and let it be instructive to the other approaches.

With your management career anchor in mind, sit down with a tablet—paper or electronic—in a quiet place and summon your sometimes distant memories of past accomplishments. Challenge yourself to list at least twenty-five accomplishments. This is for you, not for anybody else. You are not trying to impress anybody. You are trying to remember your successes that build confidence. It does not have to be done in one sitting.

Please don't think you can fully tap into your past successes by dialoguing with somebody else. You will come up short. Very shortly, you'll be trying to impress, not remember.

When you freely list all your accomplishments, you'll be surprised at what you uncover. One manager smiled as he remembered his first job as a paperboy and the discipline he learned from it. You'll become self-directed, not other-directed. As Beth Milwid, PhD, once advised me, "Sometimes, you have to go slow to go fast."

My Accomplishments

Confidence is success remembered.

_____
_____
_____
_____
_____
_____
_____
_____
_____
_____
_____
_____
_____
_____
_____
_____
_____
_____
_____
_____
_____
_____
_____
_____
_____
_____
_____
_____
_____
_____
_____
_____
_____
_____
_____

Take a deep breath. How did that go?

If you are like most managers we've have worked with over the years, you probably were able to list the first twelve to fourteen, maybe sixteen to eighteen, accomplishments fairly easily, but the next batch was more challenging. It is in that second batch of successes that the value of the activity is realized. Let it settle. See your successes. Be inspired to be more confident and focused.

More Decisions!

You'll now have to choose your top three to five accomplishments to be used in your resume, using whatever sorting process and criteria you're comfortable with. Not that easy, is it? But isn't that what the practice of management is all about—sorting information and making hard decisions?

With your key accomplishments fresh in front of you, you'll need to bring them back to your consciousness by applying what I like to call CPR. No, this is not the clinical CPR process used as an emergency lifesaving procedure in health care. This is your career CPR process. It speaks to your conditions, performance, and results. It works by asking yourself the following three questions:

1. What were the *conditions/circumstances* (C) under which I operated? Did I initiate an idea? Was I chosen to lead a project? Was there time pressure? Did I have to relate to senior management or other peer departments or functions?
2. What about your *performance* (P)? What action did you take? What did you do—did you analyze, design, teach, supervise, and maintain a good attendance record? Did you receive any recognition for what you accomplished?
3. What *results* (R) were realized? Were your customers more satisfied? Did sales go up? Were expenses reduced? Was teamwork enhanced? Were innovative ideas surfaced? Were your team members more customer-focused?

When you do CPR on your accomplishments, your attitude will automatically become more positive. You will begin to see the unique service you have provided to previous employers under a diverse set of circumstances. If you were successful under these conditions, it is predictive that you will be successful when a new, future challenge comes along.

This attitude of success is what you want to convey to yourself and to future audiences when a new opportunity arises. Do a good job here, and you build a solid foundation for successful career management and transitioning. Do a poor job here, and your foundation may crumble when you need it most.

My revived accomplishments

conditions

performance

results

My revived accomplishments

conditions

performance

results

My revived accomplishments

conditions

performance

results

Now it's time to take those three to five key achievements and format them into an attention-getting profile or qualification summary.

Based on my accomplishments, I would describe myself as_____

_____

_____

_____

_____

_____

_____

_____

_____

_____

_____

_____

_____

This is your profile. It should be interesting and attention-grabbing so busy professionals in search of talent will take the time to read it. It will be a brief snapshot of you–your career identity.

Building excitement in print:
paper or electronic

Name address phone number email address
(Makes contact easy)

PROFILE
(Gains attention and arouses interest)

Professional Accomplishments
(Builds credibility)

Professional Experience
(Provides context)

Education, Awards, Writings
(Distinguishes you from others)

With your pattern of career accomplishments fresh in your mind, what if you meet somebody new who asks, "What do you do for a living?" How would you respond? Write your answer here.

_____

_____

_____

_____

_____

_____

_____

_____

_____

_____

Did you respond in terms of *features*—a description of yourself as a manager—or in terms of *benefits*—what you do for your organization, such as, "I develop organizational capability to resolve today's and tomorrow's challenges"? Consider the benefits you provide/have provided to your customers over the years.

The following are some examples of personal benefit statements:

- I'm a supervisor/foreman. I'm the person who makes it all happen for the organization. I pull it all together and make sure a quality product goes out the door, on time. I motivate people, give technical advice, hold costs down, provide my superiors with accurate customer insight and production information, and inform my superiors when I see a possible problem.
- I am a manager. I'm the backbone of my organization. I develop organizational capability to resolve today's and tomorrow's challenges. I interact with employees and keep their eyes on the big picture while managing many of the smaller parts. I develop teams. I coordinate with other functions. I keep my superiors aware of possible technical, financial, social, and customer furtherance issues and future economic opportunities.

Write your personal benefit statement here.

_____

_____

_____

_____

_____

_____

_____

_____

_____

_____

_____

_____

Do these things to stay prepared and be a better manager, a better contributor, and a better manager of change.

OK, let's take time to review, reflect, and reform your progress in creating your living résumé. You have done the following:

- refocused your attitude to an affirmative one of *I am managing my career*
- clarified your key accomplishments
- formatted your accomplishments for easy reading, showing features and contributions to organizational capability
- written a personal benefit statement as a daily reminder of how you contributed to organizational capability

With this done, let's turn our attention to completing the process of making your résumé your living résumé:

- Share it with the people who make up your significant support system.
- Put it in your top drawer.
- Update it frequently: review, reflect, reform.

- Remember: résumé creation is a process, not an event.

Keep on living your management career. Whatever your station, labors, and aspirations, management is a noble profession that builds worth for you, your family, your stakeholders, and your organization. Enjoy the journey.

CHAPTER 7

Creating New Ways to Contribute

— ❧ —

Don't wait for the right opportunity: create it.
—George Bernard Shaw

On occasion, I like to send my young granddaughter a riddle to get her to smile—and to think. It's my small contribution to her growth. She liked this one:

Q: A young girl fell off a twenty-foot ladder but did not get hurt. Why?

A: She was standing on the first rung.

My granddaughter's response was, "Ohhh, ha, ha, ha, ha. That's good!"

A riddle is a question or statement intentionally phrased so as to require one to see a problem or a statement in a new way to discover its answer or meaning. Try these:

Q: I have cities, but no houses. I have mountains, but no trees. I have water, but no fish. What am I?

A: A map.

Q: You see a boat filled with people. It has not sunk, but when you look again, you don't see a single person on the boat. Why?

A: All the people are married.

How about a management riddle?

Q: A manager was downsized but did not lose ground in her career. Why?

A: She was standing on firm ground.

The manager saw her anchor as a career she managed, the success of which was measured by the organizational capability she created in her wake. Acknowledging her contribution to her organization's current and future worth gave her confidence. She took personal responsibility to manage herself. She was prepared!

She saw organizational capability as something that is always needed but rarely measured. She saw opportunity where others didn't. It was hidden in the work she did. Her response was, "Ohhh, ha, ha, ha, ha. That's good!" She looked for what she could give, not what she could get.

Unbeknownst to her, she was following a thoughtway going back at least to the 1800s and probably before, the theme of which is that opportunity lurks in everyone's backyard.

It was a thoughtway popularized by Dr. Russell Conwell, the founder of Temple University, who took to heart the lesson he heard from an old guide hired to take him down the Tigers and Euphrates rivers. He made it his own and would go on to tell that story some six thousand times, localizing it as he went along. It was not just a great story to tell. It was a fact of life found in town after town around the world.

His story was entitled "Acres of Diamonds." Perhaps you have read it. The story goes as follows:

> There once lived a man not far from the River Indus, an ancient Persian by the name of Al Hafed.
>
> Al Hafed owned a very large farm. He had orchards, grain-fields, and gardens. He was a wealthy and apparently contented man until one day a Buddhist priest came to visit.
>
> He sat down by the fire and told Hafed about diamonds that were so amazing that one diamond the size of his thumb could purchase the country.
>
> When Al Hafed heard all about these diamonds and how much they were worth, he went to bed that night feeling like a poor man.

He hadn't lost anything, but he felt poor because he was discontented and discontented because he thought he was poor.

The more he lay awake, the more he wanted those diamonds.

In the morning he found the priest and said, "Will you tell me where I can find diamonds? I want to be immensely rich."

"Well, then go along and find them. That is all you have to do; go and find them, and then you will have them."

"But I don't know where to go."

"Well, if you find a river that runs through white sands, between high mountains, in those white sands you will always find diamonds."

Then Al Hafed said, "I will go."

So he sold his farm and collected the money from the sale. He left his family to be taken care of by a neighbor and then away he went in search of diamonds.

He began his search at the Mountains of the Moon, but he had no luck there.

Later he searched in Palestine. Then he wandered on into Europe, and finally, when his money was gone and he was in rags, he ended up in Spain.

He was feeling hopeless, because his search for diamonds produced nothing. But that wasn't the only reason he was feeling hopeless. He was feeling hopeless because in the process of searching for the diamonds he had spent all his wealth.

In Spain, he stood on the shore of the bay to Barcelona watching a great wave as it came rolling in between the Pillars of Hercules.

He felt so hopeless that he finally could no longer resist the awful temptation to throw himself into that incoming tide.

And so he did and he sank quickly to his death beneath its foaming crest of water.

The old guide then told Dr. Conwell that the man who purchased Al Hafed's farm one day led his camel into the garden to drink.

As that camel put its nose into the shallow water of that garden brook, Al Hafed's successor noticed a curious flash of light from the white sands of the stream. He pulled out a black stone having an eye of light reflecting all the hues of the rainbow.

He took the stone into the house and put it on the mantel which covers the central fires and then he forgot all about it.

A few days later the same old priest who had visited Al Hafed came to visit the new owner of the land.

The moment Al Hafed's successor opened the door and the priest saw that flash of light on the mantel, he rushed up to it and shouted, "Here is a diamond! Has Al Hafed returned?"

The new owner of the property replied, "Oh no! Al Hafed has not returned and that is not a diamond. That is nothing but a stone we found right out here in our garden."

The priest protested, "But I know a diamond when I see it. I am sure that is a diamond!"

As the impact of that statement hit them, they both realized what that meant. It meant the stream on the property contained diamonds.

When they realized this, they rushed out into that old garden and stirred up the white sands with their fingers.

And, as unbelievable as it sounds, they discovered other even more other beautiful and valuable gems than the first.

At this point in the story the guide looked Dr. Conwell in the eye and said "That is how they discovered the diamond mine of Golconda, the most magnificent diamond mine in all history."

Almost as if on cue, the old guide took off his hat, and waved it in the air and then announced the moral of the story. "Had Al Hafed remained at home and dug in his own cellar, or underneath this own wheat fields, or in his own garden instead of wretchedness, starvation, and death he would have acres of diamonds."

What is the moral of this story for practicing managers? It is quite simply this: you can have your own figurative acres of diamonds if you prospect in your own backyard and unearth opportunities that exist in your organization right now. Regularly ask yourself the following key questions:

- Can I call myself a first-class manager?
- Do I know all I can about my industry?
- Do I know all I can about my customer?
- Do I know all I can about my employees?
- How will management be performed ten years from now?
- Do I know my own backyard and its many domains?
    o community domain
    o financial domain
    o spiritual domain
    o home and family domain
    o social domain
    o career anchor domain
    o health domain
    o personal development (administrative) domain

Mahatma Gandhi wrote, "Life is one indivisible whole." And it has never been so true as in tending your own garden. You have chosen people of good character to live with and do business with in all your domains. Build those relationships. Reach out to them. Build a reputation for asking questions. Ask about their struggles to build their organizational capability.

Listen and learn from others. Build relationships. Don't just conduct transactions. It has been said that when we leave school, people become our textbooks. Read them, listen to them, and learn from them.

Be curious about the people in those other domains, from your inner circle to the next ring out to the third ring out. Which domains could benefit from your talents of organization and insight? What excites you? You'll have so many opportunities to choose from.

How do we know when a seemingly great opportunity is not right for us? First, think about how it relates to your purpose. Do your research before going for it; look for red flags. Seek advice from those with different experiences. Don't be pressured by the *shoulds*. See future trends. You'll know it's time to say no when you notice the following:

- You know you can't deliver.
- Long term-costs outweigh short-term benefits.
- You are already stretched too thin.

- Nothing about it excites you.
- You are clearly being taken advantage of.

Here is a final riddle for you.

Q: What is always there in every organization but often missed?

A: An opportunity to contribute hidden in the work we do—technically, financially, socially, and with customers.

Why not search for it from your inner circle out?

CHAPTER 8

Living Your Legacy

·⧒·

> It is the customer who determines what a business is. For it is the customer, and he alone, who through being willing to pay for a good or service, converts economic resources into wealth, things into goods.
> —Peter Drucker, *The Practice of Management* (1954)

From my introductory story of that Philadelphia foreman, it has been my intent to put the above thought into context for practicing managers— the men and women who chose management as their career and whose success is measured by the organizational capability they create in their wake.

Warren Buffett has said that one of the key factors he looks for when evaluating an organization is the competency of the organization's "solid management team"—a team, we would say, that grows organizational capability.

Your practice is at the heart of your organization's solid management team. It challenges you, as John Holland challenged me so many years ago, to "manage thyself" no matter the stage of your career and the life cycle of your organization.

We think of legacy as a result, not a goal. It is the result of a career-long practice of creating and furthering a customer mindset in your employees and fellow managers by choosing to do tasks that result in organizational capability. The issues of tasks and purpose are not separate but rather associated with one another. Tasks flow naturally from purpose.

This process reminds me of the classic thought experiment attributed to George Berkeley, who in the eighteenth century asked, "If a tree falls in a forest and nobody is there to hear it, does it make a sound?" It raises questions about observation and perception. To answer the question adequately, we need to understand context and define our terms.

For example, is *sound* a vibration or an actual activity? We see it as an actual activity when sound is defined as a particular auditory impression—the sensation perceived by the sense of hearing. Once so defined, it has focus and direction.

This creates an implied a relationship between sound and a person. If there is not a person to hear it, the sound of a falling tree does not exist. Sound is the product of our ears; if there are no membranes to vibrate, then there is no sound. We see it as an actual activity.

Now, let's consider a thought experiment in an organizational context: If a manager walks out of the office each night, each year, and at the end of a long career has compiled a record of successes yet leaves no organizational capability, no long-term impact on others, did management occur? To answer the question, we need once again to understand context and define our terms.

Is management a vibration or an actual activity? We see it as an actual activity, a practice. We have defined management as a career, the success of which is defined by the organizational capability we create in our wake. Once so defined, it has a unique focus and direction.

This creates an implied relationship between the practice of management and the future of one's organization. We contend that if the organization does not grow in capability, no management occurs— no organizational capability, no management, and a declining future sustainability.

Legacy

Legacy is an important component of management. It puts a stamp on the future; it makes a contribution to future generations. We need to change the notion of legacy to something that is not only celebrated at the end of one's career but is passed along throughout one's career.

This is not a new idea. In 1889, Andrew Carnegie, in an article directed to the wealthy of his generation, wrote, "They have it in their power during their lives to busy themselves in organizing benefactions from which the masses of their fellows will derive lasting advantage, and thus dignify their own lives."

As a practicing manager, you have it within your power during your career to busy yourself about organizing activities from which others will derive lasting advantage and thus dignify your own life. If we expand our understanding of wealth beyond the traditional, we can begin to appreciate how legacy applies to organizational capability and the knowledge, skills, and attitudes of practicing managers.

Wealth has several meanings, including an abundance of valuable possessions or money, as well as the plentiful supplies of a particular resource. Your organization's unique knowledge is one such resource. From an organizational perspective, knowledge can be seen as the product of a learning subsystem that facilitates the pursuit of purposeful performance, where employees are engaged in seeking knowledge about the work they do, for whom they do it, and how it contributes to sustaining their organization. It is in this expanded view of what work is, for whom it is done, the importance of organizational capability, and the meaning of legacy that I offer my thoughts on how practicing managers can build clarity in their organization, their management team, and their employees, thereby dignifying their career.

Today, many senior-level managers in organizations of all sizes and types are influenced by what Roger Mougalas called *big data*—extremely large data sets that can be analyzed computationally to reveal patterns, trends, and associations, and to spot business trends, prevent diseases, combat crime, and so on depending on the organization. It is a relative term.

At the operational level, practicing managers are most influenced by what we'll call *work data*—the facts and statistics collected and pulled together for reference or the analysis of performance. Remembering that work is the mental, physical, and emotional effort done for somebody else in order to achieve a purpose, I am inclined to ask: are you, as a manager, collecting and pulling together the facts and statistics of all the domains of work?

It is here, at the operational level, that practicing managers can most directly tap into their teams' realized and potential knowledge to be effective; to create curiosity and organizational capability; and to drive employee engagement. Legacy-creating opportunities exist in the system architecture and in the competency-development process. Which opportunity path you choose may depend on your mindset.

Julia Galef, cofounder of the Center for Applied Rationality, gives practicing managers a good metaphor for understanding these two paths. She refers to them as the *soldier* mindset and the *scout* mindset.

The soldier mindset, she explains, stems from their soldiers' ingrained need to protect themselves and their side and to defeat the enemy. In organizational complexity, some pieces of information feel like our allies. We want them to win; we want to defend them. Other pieces of information are the enemy, and we want to shoot them down.

The scout's job, in contrast, is not to attack or defend; it's to understand. The scout is going out, mapping the terrain, and identifying potential obstacles. Above all, the scout wants to know what's really out there as accurately as possible.

In an actual army, both the solider and the scout are essential. In the actual practice of one's management career, one is asked to be both soldier and scout. Do like a soldier. Think like a scout. Evolve your legacy. Contribute to the architecture and competencies of pursuing purposeful performance that grows organizational capability.

Galef ends her case with a quote from *The Little Prince* to inspire both the soldier and the scout—and, from our perspective, the practicing manager: "If you want to build a ship, don't drum up your men to collect wood and give orders and distribute the work. Instead, teach them to yearn for the vast and endless sea."

If you want to live a legacy of developing organizational capability that will ensure the sustainability of your organization, don't drum up your men to collect wood and give orders and distribute the work. Instead, teach them to yearn for the vast and endless opportunities awaiting them in creating and furthering their customer.

ABOUT THE AUTHOR

After earning a bachelor's degree in economics and sociology from St. Francis University, Patrick Olliffe went to work to find what contributions he could make in the world of work. Attendance at the US Army's Instructor Training Program in Ft. Knox, Kentucky, would give him a focus and direction that would last throughout his career. Field manuals, his captain told him, would give him the subject knowledge he needed; understanding would come from interviewing the practicing experts about the situational conditions they faced. Respect for his attendees was drilled into him.

Consulting experience in multiple industries across the United States and into Canada, with APC Skills and the Institute of Management Resources, would give breadth and depth to his work as he continued to connect operations and management training into an seamless change initiative. It was at USAirway's maintenance division, where he worked as director of administration, that he developed a cost-effective, work-centric approach to developing managers. This began with identifying areas of excessive costs, investigating the practices that were perpetuating them, and—in conjunction with senior leadership—finding ways to control them while growing management competencies and building organizational capability.

At R. Davenport and Associates, Patrick would again build on what they had to expand client outplacement services while building management competencies and organizational capability in a challenging time. His inquisitiveness, study, and blended work experiences continue to inspire him to advance the value of organizational capability in organizations and career management in individual managers.

SUGGESTED READING

Acres of Diamonds by Russell Conwell (1890)

Beyond Measure by Margaret Hefferman (2015)

Career Anchors by Edgar Schein (2006)

Closing the Engagement Gap by Julie Gebauer and Don Lowman (2008)

Corporate Lifecycles by Ichak Adizes (1987)

Cross-Functional Teams by Glenn Parker (1994)

Five Minds for the Future by Howard Gardner (2006)

How to Win Friends and Influence People by Dale Carnegie (1975)

Human Competence by Thomas Gilbert (1978)

If Disney Ran Your Hospital by Fred Lee (2004)

Leader Effective Training by Dr. Thomas Gordon (1977)

Learning from Work by Anne Beamish (2008)

Management of Organizational Behavior by Paul Hersey and Kenneth Blanchard (1967)

Managing through People by Dale Carnegie and Associates (1975)

Polarity Management by Barry Johnson, PhD (1992)

Re-Engineering the Corporation by Michael Hammer and James Champy (1993)

Service America by Karl Albrecht (1985)

Start with Why by Simon Sinek (2009)

The Adult Learner: A Neglected Species by Malcolm Knowles (1973)

The Customer Comes Second by Hal Rosenbluth (2002)

The Evolution of Everything by Matt Ridley (2015)

The Experience Economy by Joseph Pine (1999)

The Five Dysfunctions of a Team by Patrick Lencioni (2002)

The Gospel of Wealth by Andrew Carnegie (1898)

The Great Game of Business by Jack Stack (1992)

The Lifetime Career Manager by James Cabrera and Charles Albrecht, Jr. (1995)

The Path of Least Resistance for Managers by Robert Fritz (1989)

The Practice of Management by Peter Drucker (1954)

Theory Z by William Ouchi (1981)

Transforming the Way We Work by Edward Marshall (1995)

What Got You Here Won't Get You There by Marshall Goldsmith (2007)

INDEX

O

organizational capability vii, ix–x, 2–9,
    11–12, 19–23, 26, 30, 33–34,
    36, 38, 43, 54–55, 58, 62,
    64–69
organizational reputation 18–19
organizational work 2

P

partner vii, xi,
personal benefit statement 54–55
practice of modern management 1
predictive self 12, 15
problem-solving 22, 25–26, 37
profile 52–53
pursuing purposeful performance
    6, 67

R

reasonable expectations 22–23, 25
reputation 18–19, 21, 25–28, 33–34,
    39–40, 62
riddles 57, 63
Robert Katz 34, 36

S

secret of the ages 17
simplicity 7
Sir Thomas More 1
someone to chase 11–12, 43
strategic way 44
Sun Tzu 31

T

tactical way 44
talent waste 31
team development 7
three bricklayers 32
time management 16
Tuckman's model 7

V

value vii, 5, 7–8, 11, 23, 36, 47, 69
voting technology 36

W

Warren Buffett 4, 64
workarounds x
work data 67

Y

your performance system 21

Printed in the United States
by Baker & Taylor Publisher Services